Cupcakes

Cupcakes

This edition published in 2012
LOVE FOOD is an imprint of Parragon Books Ltd

Parragon
Queen Street House
4 Queen Street
Bath BA1 1HE, UK

Copyright © Parragon Books Ltd 2010

www.parragon.com/lovefood

ISBN: 978-1-4454-8745-8

Printed in China

Notes for the Reader
This book uses both metric and imperial measurements. Follow the same units of
measurement throughout; do not mix metric and imperial. All spoon measurements are
level: teaspoons are assumed to be 5 ml, and tablespoons are assumed to be 15 ml. Unless
otherwise stated, milk is assumed to be full fat, eggs and individual vegetables are medium,
and pepper is freshly ground black pepper.

The times given are an approximate guide only. Preparation times differ according to the
techniques used by different people and the cooking times may also vary from those
given. Optional ingredients, variations or serving suggestions have not been included in the
calculations.

Recipes using raw or very lightly cooked eggs should be avoided by infants, the elderly,
pregnant women, convalescents and anyone suffering from an illness. Pregnant and
breastfeeding women are advised to avoid eating peanuts and peanut products. Sufferers
from nut allergies should be aware that some of the ready-made ingredients used in the
recipes in this book may contain nuts. Always check the packaging before use.

Contents

Introduction

Who can resist a cupcake? These diminutive cakes are loved by all and are the perfect little treat to indulge in at any time. They are easy to make, fun, pretty and add that little touch of extravagance to any event, from a birthday to Christmas and even weddings.

This book is full of tempting ideas to treat yourself, family and friends and includes classic cupcakes through to more elaborate recipes to ensure you're never short of ideas for these irresistible and individual cakes.

Baking is a science as well as an art, so it is important to follow the recipes precisely. Before you start, read through the recipe and gather together all of the required ingredients and equipment. Specialist equipment is not necessary as most kitchens will have the essentials; these are measuring scales, mixing bowls, a wooden spoon, baking trays and bun tins. Buying the correct cases is also important as they help retain that characteristic cupcake shape but also help keep them fresh and moist. Fluted paper or foil baking cases are perfect but you can also now buy reusable, silicone cases that are brightly coloured and do the job just as well.

Follow the top tips on the opposite page to ensure perfect results and you'll soon realize there is no time like the present to dig out your apron, get baking and rediscover the joy of baking a batch of cupcake delights!

• Turn on the oven before you start in order to preheat it to the correct temperature while you're mixing.

• Use the baking times for each recipe as a guideline only. Temperatures vary widely from appliance to appliance. Being aware of this will ensure the best results every time.

• Always use eggs at room temperature. If you store eggs in the refrigerator, remove them about 30 minutes before use to allow them to come up to room temperature.

• Avoid over-mixing because this can cause a heavy texture – beat the mixture until just smooth.

• Bake the cupcakes immediately once mixed because the raising agents begin to act as soon as they're combined with liquid.

• Avoid opening the oven during cooking – this reduces the oven temperature and can cause the cupcakes to sink. Do however check just a few minutes before the end of the baking time to see how the cupcakes are progressing.

• Test for doneness – the cupcakes should be well risen and springy to the touch.

Everyday Cupcakes

Lemon Butterfly Cakes

makes 12

115 g/4 oz self-raising flour
½ tsp baking powder
115 g/4 oz butter, softened,
or soft margarine
115 g/4 oz caster sugar
2 eggs
finely grated rind of
½ lemon
2 tbsp milk

frosting
85 g/3 oz butter, softened
175 g/6 oz icing sugar
1 tbsp lemon juice

Preheat the oven to 190°C/375°F/Gas Mark 5. Put 12 paper baking cases in a bun tin or put 12 double-layer paper cases on a baking tray.

Sift the flour and baking powder into a large bowl, add the butter, sugar, eggs, lemon rind and milk and beat together until smooth. Spoon the mixture into the paper cases.

Bake in the preheated oven for 15–20 minutes, or until well risen and springy to the touch. Transfer to a wire rack to cool completely.

To make the frosting, place the butter in a bowl and beat until light and fluffy. Sift in the icing sugar, add the lemon juice and beat together until smooth and creamy. When the cupcakes are cold, cut the top off each cake then cut the top in half.

Spread or pipe a little of the lemon frosting over the cut surface of each cupcake, then gently press the 2 cut cake pieces into it at an angle to resemble butterfly wings.

Rose Petal Cupcakes

makes 12

115 g/4 oz butter, softened
115 g/4 oz caster sugar
2 eggs, lightly beaten
1 tbsp milk
few drops of essence of rose oil
¼ tsp vanilla extract
175 g/6 oz self-raising flour
silver dragées, to decorate

crystallized rose petals
12–24 rose petals
lightly beaten egg white, for brushing
caster sugar, for sprinkling

frosting
85 g/3 oz butter, softened
175 g/6 oz icing sugar
pink or purple food colouring (optional)

To make the crystallized rose petals, gently rinse the petals and dry well with kitchen paper. Using a pastry brush, paint both sides of a rose petal with egg white, then coat well with caster sugar. Place on a tray and repeat with the remaining petals. Cover the tray with foil and leave overnight.

Preheat the oven to 200°C/400°F/Gas Mark 6. Put 12 paper baking cases in a bun tin or put 12 double-layer paper cases on a baking tray.

Place the butter and sugar in a large bowl and beat together until light and fluffy, then gradually beat in the eggs. Stir in the milk, rose essence and vanilla extract, then fold in the flour. Spoon the mixture into the paper cases.

Bake in the preheated oven for 12–15 minutes, or until well risen and springy to the touch. Transfer to a wire rack to cool completely.

To make the frosting, place the butter in a large bowl and beat until light and fluffy. Sift in the icing sugar and mix well together. Add a few drops of pink or purple food colouring to match the rose petals, if liked.

When the cupcakes are cold, spread the frosting on top of each cake. Top with 1–2 crystallized rose petals and sprinkle with silver dragées.

Banoffee Cupcakes

makes 4

100 g/3½ oz butter, softened, plus extra for greasing

100 g/3½ oz soft light brown sugar

2 eggs, lightly beaten

100 g/3½ oz self-raising flour

1 small ripe banana, peeled and mashed

topping

150 ml/5 fl oz double cream

½ banana, peeled and sliced

2 tbsp dulce de leche (toffee sauce)

1 tbsp grated chocolate

Preheat the oven to 190°C/375°F/Gas Mark 5. Grease 4 x 200-ml/ 7-fl oz ovenproof teacups or dishes (such as ramekins) with butter.

Put the butter and sugar in a bowl and beat together until light and fluffy. Gradually beat in the eggs. Sift in the flour and, using a metal spoon, fold into the mixture with the mashed banana. Spoon the mixture into the cups or dishes.

Put the teacups or dishes on a baking sheet and bake in the preheated oven for 20–25 minutes, or until well risen and golden brown. Transfer to a wire rack to cool completely.

For the topping, whisk the cream in a bowl until softly peaking. Spoon the whipped cream on top of each cupcake then arrange 3–4 banana slices on top. Drizzle over the dulce de leche and sprinkle over the grated chocolate. Store the cupcakes in the refrigerator until ready to serve.

Chewy Flapjack Cupcakes

makes 8

55 g/2 oz butter, softened
55 g/2 oz golden caster sugar
1 large egg, lightly beaten
55 g/2 oz self-raising flour

topping
40 g/1½ oz soft tub margarine
40 g/1½ oz demerara sugar
1 tbsp golden syrup
55 g/2 oz rolled oats

Preheat the oven to 190°C/375°F/Gas Mark 5. Put 8 paper baking cases in a bun tin or put 8 double-layer paper cases on a baking tray.

To make the flapjack topping, place the margarine, demerara sugar and golden syrup in a small saucepan and heat gently until the margarine has melted. Stir in the oats. Set aside.

Put the butter and sugar in a bowl and beat together until light and fluffy. Gradually beat in the egg. Sift in the flour and, using a metal spoon, fold gently into the mixture. Spoon the mixture into the paper cases. Gently spoon the flapjack mixture over the top.

Bake in the preheated oven for 20 minutes, or until well risen and the topping is golden brown. Transfer to a wire rack to cool completely.

Iced Fairy Cakes

makes 16

115 g/4 oz butter, softened
115 g/4 oz caster sugar
2 eggs, lightly beaten
115 g/4 oz self-raising flour
sugar flowers, hundreds and
thousands, glacé cherries and/
or chocolate strands,
to decorate

icing
200 g/7 oz icing sugar
about 2 tbsp warm water
a few drops of food colouring
(optional)

Preheat the oven to 190°C/375°F/Gas Mark 5. Put 16 paper baking cases in 2 x 12-hole bun tins or put 16 double-layer paper cases on a baking tray.

Place the butter and sugar in a large bowl and beat together until light and fluffy, then gradually beat in the eggs. Sift in the flour and fold into the mixture. Spoon the mixture into the paper cases.

Bake in the preheated oven for 15–20 minutes, or until well risen and springy to the touch. Transfer to a wire rack to cool completely.

To make the icing, sift the icing sugar into a bowl and stir in just enough warm water to mix to a smooth paste that is thick enough to coat the back of a wooden spoon. Stir in a few drops of food colouring, if using, then spread the icing over the fairy cakes and decorate, as liked.

Queen Cakes

makes 18

115 g/4 oz butter, softened, or soft margarine

115 g/4 oz caster sugar

2 large eggs, lightly beaten

4 tsp lemon juice

175 g/6 oz self-raising flour

115 g/4 oz currants

2–4 tbsp milk, if necessary

Preheat the oven to 190°C/375°F/Gas Mark 5. Put 18 paper baking cases in 2 x 12-hole bun tins or put 18 double-layer paper cases on a baking tray.

Place the butter and sugar in a large bowl and beat together until light and fluffy. Gradually beat in the eggs, then beat in the lemon juice with 1 tablespoon of the flour. Fold in the remaining flour and the currants. If necessary, add a little milk to give a soft dropping consistency. Spoon the mixture into the paper cases.

Bake in the preheated oven for 15–20 minutes, or until well risen and springy to the touch. Transfer to a wire rack to cool completely.

Rocky Road Cupcakes

makes 12

2 tbsp cocoa powder

2 tbsp hot water

115 g/4 oz butter, softened

115 g/4 oz caster sugar

2 eggs, lightly beaten

115 g/4 oz self-raising flour

topping

25 g/1 oz chopped mixed nuts

100 g/3½ oz milk chocolate, melted

115 g/4 oz mini marshmallows

40 g/1½ oz glacé cherries, chopped

Preheat the oven to 180°C/350°F/Gas Mark 4. Put 12 paper muffin cases in a muffin tin or put 12 double-layer paper cases on a baking tray.

Blend the cocoa powder and hot water together and set aside. Put the butter and sugar in a bowl and beat together until light and fluffy. Gradually beat in the eggs, then beat in the blended cocoa. Sift in the flour and, using a metal spoon, fold gently into the mixture. Spoon the mixture into the paper cases.

Bake in the preheated oven for 20 minutes, or until well risen and springy to the touch. Transfer to a wire rack to cool completely.

To make the topping, stir the nuts into the melted chocolate and spread a little of the mixture over the top of the cakes. Lightly stir the marshmallows and cherries into the remaining chocolate mixture and pile on top of the cupcakes. Leave to set.

Double Ginger Cupcakes

makes 12

175 g/6 oz plain flour
1 tbsp baking powder
2 tsp ground ginger
175 g/6 oz unsalted butter,
softened
175 g/6 oz light muscovado
sugar
3 eggs, beaten
25 g/1 oz crystallized stem
ginger, finely chopped
diced crystallized ginger,
to decorate

frosting

200 g/7 oz ricotta cheese
85 g/3 oz icing sugar, sifted
finely grated rind of
1 tangerine

Preheat the oven to 190°C/375°F/Gas Mark 5. Put 12 paper baking cases in a bun tin or put 12 double-layer paper cases on a baking tray.

Sift the flour, baking powder and ground ginger into a large bowl. Add the butter, muscovado sugar and eggs and beat well until smooth. Stir in the crystallized stem ginger.

Spoon the mixture into the paper cases. Bake in the preheated oven for 15–20 minutes, or until well risen and springy to the touch. Transfer to a wire rack to cool completely.

For the frosting, mix together the ricotta, icing sugar and tangerine rind until smooth. Spoon a little frosting onto each cupcake and spread over the surface to cover. Decorate with the diced crystallized ginger and leave to set.

Moist Walnut Cupcakes

makes 12

85 g/3 oz walnuts
55 g/2 oz butter, softened, cut into small pieces
100 g/3½ oz caster sugar
grated rind of ½ lemon
70 g/2½ oz self-raising flour
2 eggs
12 walnut halves, to decorate

frosting
55 g/2 oz butter, softened
85 g/3 oz icing sugar
grated rind of ½ lemon
1 tsp lemon juice

Preheat the oven to 190°C/375°F/Gas Mark 5. Put 12 paper baking cases in a bun tin or put 12 double-layer paper cases on a baking tray.

Place the walnuts in a food processor and pulse until finely ground. Be careful not to overgrind, as the nuts will turn to oil.

Add the butter, caster sugar, lemon rind, flour and eggs and blend until the mixture is evenly combined. Spoon the mixture into the paper cases.

Bake in the preheated oven for 20 minutes, or until well risen and springy to the touch. Transfer to a wire rack to cool completely.

To make the frosting, place the butter in a bowl and beat together until light and fluffy. Sift in the icing sugar, add the lemon rind and juice and mix well together. When the cupcakes are cold, spread the frosting on top of each cupcake and top with a walnut half to decorate.

Frosted Peanut Butter Cupcakes

makes 16

55 g/2 oz butter, softened, or
soft margarine

225 g/8 oz soft light brown
sugar

115 g/4 oz crunchy peanut
butter

2 eggs, lightly beaten

1 tsp vanilla extract

225 g/8 oz plain flour

2 tsp baking powder

100 ml/3½ fl oz milk

frosting

200 g/7 oz full-fat soft cream
cheese

25 g/1 oz butter, softened

225 g/8 oz icing sugar

Preheat the oven to 180°C/350°F/Gas Mark 4. Put 16 paper muffin cases in 2 x 12-hole muffin tins or put 16 double-layer paper cases on a baking tray.

Place the butter, sugar and peanut butter in a bowl and beat together for 1–2 minutes, or until well mixed. Gradually beat in the eggs, then add the vanilla extract. Sift in the flour and baking powder, then fold them into the mixture, alternating with the milk. Spoon the mixture into the paper cases.

Bake in the preheated oven for 25 minutes, or until well risen and springy to the touch. Transfer to a wire rack to cool completely.

To make the frosting, place the cream cheese and butter in a large bowl and beat together until smooth. Sift the icing sugar into the mixture, beat together until well mixed, then spread the frosting on top of each cupcake.

Chocolate Box

Jumbo Chocolate Chip Cupcakes

makes 8

100 g/3½ oz butter, softened,
or soft margarine

100 g/3½ oz caster sugar

2 large eggs

100 g/3½ oz self-raising flour

100 g/3½ oz plain chocolate
chips

Preheat the oven to 190°C/375°F/Gas Mark 5. Put 8 paper muffin cases in a muffin tin or put 8 double-layer paper cases on a baking tray.

Place the butter, sugar, eggs and flour in a large bowl and beat together until just smooth. Fold in the chocolate chips. Spoon the mixture into the paper cases.

Bake in the preheated oven for 20–25 minutes, or until well risen and springy to the touch. Transfer to a wire rack to cool completely.

Chocolate Cupcakes with Cream Cheese Frosting

makes 10

100 g/3½ oz unsalted butter, softened, or soft margarine

100 g/3½ oz caster sugar

2 eggs, lightly beaten

100 g/3½ oz self-raising flour

15 g/½ oz cocoa powder

1 tbsp milk

55 g/2 oz plain chocolate chips

frosting

150 g/5½ oz white chocolate, broken into pieces

140 g/5 oz full-fat cream cheese

chocolate curls, to decorate

Preheat the oven to 190°C/375°F/Gas Mark 5. Line a 12-hole muffin tray with 10 paper cases.

Place the butter and sugar in a bowl and beat together until light and fluffy, then gradually beat in the eggs. Sift over the flour and cocoa powder and fold in gently. Fold in the milk and chocolate chips.

Divide the mixture between the paper cases. Bake in the preheated oven for 20 minutes, or until risen and springy to the touch. Transfer to a wire rack and leave to cool completely.

To make the frosting, place the white chocolate in a heatproof bowl set over a pan of simmering water and leave until melted. Remove from the heat, stir until smooth then leave to cool for 15 minutes. Place the cream cheese in a separate bowl and beat until smooth. Gradually beat in the melted chocolate until evenly combined.

Swirl the frosting over the top of the cupcakes and decorate with chocolate curls.

Mocha Cupcakes with Whipped Cream

makes 20

2 tbsp instant espresso coffee powder

85 g/3 oz butter

85 g/3 oz caster sugar

1 tbsp clear honey

200 ml/7 fl oz water

225 g/8 oz plain flour

2 tbsp cocoa powder

1 tsp bicarbonate of soda

3 tbsp milk

1 large egg, lightly beaten

cocoa powder, for dusting

topping

225 ml/8 fl oz whipping cream

Preheat the oven to 180°C/350°F/Gas Mark 4. Put 20 paper baking cases in 2 x 12-hole bun tins or put 20 double-layer paper cases on a baking tray.

Place the coffee powder, butter, sugar, honey and water in a saucepan and heat gently, stirring, until the sugar has dissolved. Bring to the boil, then reduce the heat and leave to simmer for 5 minutes. Pour into a large heatproof bowl and leave to cool.

When the mixture has cooled, sift in the flour and cocoa powder. Place the bicarbonate of soda and milk in a bowl and stir to dissolve, then add to the mixture with the egg and beat together until smooth. Spoon the mixture into the paper cases.

Bake in the preheated oven for 15–20 minutes, or until well risen and springy to the touch. Transfer to a wire rack to cool completely.

For the topping, place the cream in a bowl and whip until it holds its shape. Spoon heaped teaspoonfuls of cream on top of each cupcake, then dust lightly with sifted cocoa powder.

Warm Molten-centred Chocolate Cupcakes

makes 6

55 g/2 oz butter, softened, or
soft margarine
55 g/2 oz caster sugar
1 large egg
85 g/3 oz self-raising flour
1 tbsp cocoa powder
55 g/2 oz plain chocolate
icing sugar, for dusting

Preheat the oven to 190°C/375°F/Gas Mark 5. Put 6 paper baking cases in a bun tin or put 6 double-layer paper cases on a baking tray.

Place the butter, sugar, egg, flour and cocoa powder in a large bowl and beat together until just smooth. Spoon half of the mixture into the paper cases. Using a teaspoon, make an indentation in the centre of each cake. Break the chocolate into 6 even squares and place a piece in each indentation, then spoon the remaining cake mixture on top.

Bake in the preheated oven for 20 minutes, or until well risen and springy to the touch. Leave the cupcakes in the tin for 2–3 minutes before serving warm, dusted with sifted icing sugar.

Marbled Chocolate Cupcakes

makes 21

175 g/6 oz soft margarine
175 g/6 oz caster sugar
3 eggs
175 g/6 oz self-raising flour
2 tbsp milk
55 g/2 oz plain chocolate, melted

Preheat the oven to 180°C/350°F/Gas Mark 4. Put 21 paper baking cases in 2 x 12-hole bun tins or put 21 double-layer paper cases on a baking tray.

Place the margarine, sugar, eggs, flour and milk in a large bowl and beat together until just smooth.

Divide the mixture between 2 bowls. Add the melted chocolate to one and stir until mixed. Using a teaspoon, and alternating the chocolate mixture with the plain, put 4 half-teaspoons into each case.

Bake in the preheated oven for 20 minutes, or until well risen and springy to the touch. Transfer to a wire rack to cool completely.

Double Chocolate Cupcakes

makes 18

85 g/3 oz white chocolate
1 tbsp milk
115 g/4 oz self-raising flour
½ tsp baking powder
115 g/4 oz butter, softened
115 g/4 oz caster sugar
2 eggs
1 tsp vanilla extract
18 white chocolate buttons,
to decorate

topping
140 g/5 oz milk chocolate

Preheat the oven to 190°C/375°F/Gas Mark 5. Put 18 paper baking cases in 2 x 12-hole bun tins, or put 18 double-layer paper cases on a baking tray.

Break the white chocolate into a heatproof bowl and add the milk. Set the bowl over a saucepan of gently simmering water and heat until melted. Remove from the heat and stir gently until smooth.

Sift the flour and baking powder into a bowl. Add the butter, sugar, eggs and vanilla extract and, using an electric hand whisk, beat together until smooth. Fold in the melted white chocolate. Spoon the mixture into the paper cases.

Bake in the preheated oven for 20 minutes, or until well risen and springy to the touch. Transfer to a wire rack and leave to cool completely.

To make the topping, break the chocolate into a heatproof bowl and set the bowl over a saucepan of gently simmering water until melted. Cool for 5 minutes then spread over the top of the cupcakes. Decorate each cupcake with a chocolate button.

Chocolate & Orange Cupcakes

makes 16

115 g/4 oz butter, softened

115 g/4 oz golden caster sugar

finely grated rind and juice of ½ orange

2 eggs, lightly beaten

115 g/4 oz self-raising flour

25 g/1 oz plain chocolate, grated

thin strips candied orange peel, to decorate

topping

115 g/4 oz plain chocolate, broken into pieces

25 g/1 oz unsalted butter

1 tbsp golden syrup

Preheat the oven to 180°C/350°F/Gas Mark 4. Put 16 paper baking cases in 2 x 12-hole bun tins or put 16 double-layer paper cases on a baking tray.

Put the butter, sugar and orange rind in a bowl and beat together until light and fluffy. Gradually beat in the eggs. Sift in the flour and, using a metal spoon, fold gently into the mixture with the orange juice and grated chocolate. Spoon the mixture into the paper cases.

Bake the cupcakes in the preheated oven for 20 minutes, or until well risen and springy to the touch. Transfer to a wire rack to cool completely.

To make the topping, break the chocolate into a heatproof bowl and add the butter and syrup. Set the bowl over a saucepan of gently simmering water and heat until melted. Remove from the heat and stir until smooth. Cool until the topping is thick enough to spread. Spread over the cupcakes and decorate each cupcake with a few strips of candied orange peel. Leave to set.

Chocolate Fruit & Nut Crispy Cakes

makes 18

300 g/10½ oz plain chocolate, broken into pieces

150 g/5½ oz butter, cut into cubes

250 g/9 oz golden syrup

100 g/3½ oz Brazil nuts, roughly chopped

100 g/3½ oz ready-to-eat dried raisins

200 g/7 oz cornflakes

18 glacé cherries, to decorate

Put 18 paper baking cases in 2 x 12-hole bun tins or put 18 double-layer paper cases on a baking tray.

Place the chocolate, butter and golden syrup into a large saucepan and heat gently until the butter has melted and the ingredients are runny but not hot. Remove from the heat and stir until well mixed.

Add the chopped nuts and raisins to the pan and stir together until the fruit and nuts are covered in chocolate. Add the cornflakes and stir until combined.

Spoon the mixture evenly into the paper cases and top each with a glacé cherry. Leave to set in a cool place for 2–4 hours before serving.

Devil's Food Cake with Chocolate Frosting

makes 18

50 g/1¾ oz butter, softened,
or soft margarine

115 g/4 oz soft dark brown
sugar

2 large eggs

115 g/4 oz plain white flour

½ tsp bicarbonate of soda

25 g/1 oz cocoa powder

125 ml/4 fl oz soured cream

frosting
125 g/4½ oz plain chocolate,
broken into pieces

2 tbsp caster sugar

150 ml/5 fl oz soured cream

**chocolate sticks
(optional)**
100 g/3½ oz plain chocolate

Preheat the oven to 180°C/350°F/Gas Mark 4. Put 18 paper baking cases in 2 x 12-hole bun tins or put 18 double-layer paper cases on a baking tray.

Place the butter, sugar, eggs, flour, bicarbonate of soda and cocoa powder in a large bowl and beat together until just smooth. Fold in the soured cream. Spoon the mixture into the paper cases.

Bake in the preheated oven for 20 minutes, or until well risen and springy to the touch. Transfer to a wire rack to cool completely.

To make the frosting, place the chocolate in a heatproof bowl, set over a saucepan of gently simmering water and heat until melted. Leave to cool slightly, then whisk in the sugar and soured cream until combined. Spread the frosting over the tops of the cakes and chill in the refrigerator before serving.

Decorate with chocolate sticks made by shaving plain chocolate with a potato peeler, if liked.

Chocolate Butterfly Cakes

makes 12

25 g/1 oz plain chocolate, broken into pieces
125 g/4½ oz butter, softened
125 g/4½ oz caster sugar
150 g/5½ oz self-raising flour
2 large eggs
2 tbsp cocoa powder
icing sugar, for dusting

frosting
100 g/3½ oz butter, softened
225 g/8 oz icing sugar
grated rind of ½ lemon
1 tbsp lemon juice

Preheat the oven to 180°C/350°F/Gas Mark 4. Put 12 paper baking cases in a bun tin or put 12 double-layer paper cases on a baking tray.

Place the chocolate in a heatproof bowl, set the bowl over a saucepan of gently simmering water and heat until melted, then leave to cool slightly.

Place the butter, sugar, flour, eggs and cocoa powder in a large bowl and beat together until the mixture is just smooth. Beat in the melted chocolate. Spoon the mixture into the paper cases.

Bake in the preheated oven for 15 minutes, or until well risen and springy to the touch. Transfer to a wire rack to cool completely.

To make the frosting, place the butter in a bowl and beat until light and fluffy, then gradually sift in the icing sugar and beat to combine. Beat in the lemon rind, then gradually beat in the lemon juice. When the cupcakes are cold, cut the top off each cake, then cut the top in half. Spread or pipe a little of the frosting over the cut surface of each cupcake, then gently press the 2 cut cake pieces into it at an angle to resemble butterfly wings. Dust with sifted icing sugar.

Feeling Fruity

Warm Strawberry Cupcakes
Baked in a Teacup

makes 6

115 g/4 oz butter, softened,
plus extra for greasing

4 tbsp strawberry jam

115 g/4 oz caster sugar

2 eggs, lightly beaten

1 tsp vanilla extract

115 g/4 oz self-raising flour

6 whole strawberries,
to decorate

icing sugar, for dusting

Preheat the oven to 180°C/350°F/Gas Mark 4. Grease
6 x 200-ml/7-fl oz ovenproof teacups or dishes (such as
ramekins). Spoon 2 teaspoons of the strawberry jam into the
bottom of each teacup.

Place the butter and sugar in a large bowl and beat together until
light and fluffy. Gradually add the eggs, beating well after each
addition, then add the vanilla extract. Sift in the flour and fold into
the mixture. Spoon the mixture into the teacups.

Stand the cups in a roasting tin, then pour in enough hot water
to come one third up the sides of the teacups. Bake in the
preheated oven for 40 minutes, or until well risen and springy to
the touch, and a skewer, inserted in the centre, comes out clean.
If overbrowning, cover the cupcakes with a sheet of foil. Leave the
cupcakes to cool for 2–3 minutes, then carefully lift the cups from
the tin and place them on saucers.

Top each cupcake with a strawberry, then dust them with sifted
icing sugar. Serve warm.

Fresh Raspberry Cupcakes

makes 12

275 g/9¾ oz fresh raspberries
150 ml/5 fl oz sunflower oil
2 eggs
140 g/5 oz caster sugar
½ tsp vanilla extract
275 g/9¾ oz plain flour
¾ tsp bicarbonate of soda
12 fresh raspberries, small
mint leaves, to decorate

topping
150 ml/5 fl oz double cream

Preheat the oven to 180°C/350°F/Gas Mark 4. Put 12 paper baking cases in a bun tin or put 12 double-layer paper cases on a baking tray.

Place the raspberries in a large bowl and crush lightly with a fork.

Place the oil, eggs, sugar and vanilla extract in a large bowl and whisk together until well combined. Sift in the flour and bicarbonate of soda and fold into the mixture, then fold in the crushed raspberries. Spoon the mixture into the paper cases.

Bake in the preheated oven for 30 minutes, or until well risen and springy to the touch. Leave the cupcakes to cool in the tin for 10 minutes, then transfer to a wire rack to cool completely.

When ready to decorate, place the cream in a bowl and whip until soft peaks form. Spread the cream on top of the cupcakes, using a knife to smooth the cream. Top each cupcake with a raspberry and decorate with mint leaves.

Apple Streusel Cupcakes

makes 14

½ tsp bicarbonate of soda

280 g/10 oz jar Bramley apple sauce

55 g/2 oz butter, softened, or soft margarine

85 g/3 oz demerara sugar

1 large egg, lightly beaten

175 g/6 oz self-raising flour

½ tsp ground cinnamon

½ tsp freshly ground nutmeg

topping

50 g/1¾ oz plain white flour

50 g/1¾ oz demerara sugar

¼ tsp ground cinnamon

¼ tsp freshly grated nutmeg

35 g/1¼ oz butter, cut into small pieces

Preheat the oven to 180°C/350°F/Gas Mark 4. Put 14 paper baking cases in 2 x 12-hole bun tins or put 14 double-layer paper cases in a baking tray.

First, make the topping. Place the flour, sugar, cinnamon and nutmeg in a large bowl. Add the butter and rub it in with your fingertips until the mixture resembles fine breadcrumbs. Reserve until required.

To make the cupcakes, add the bicarbonate of soda to the jar of apple sauce and stir until dissolved. Place the butter and sugar in a large bowl and beat together until light and fluffy, then gradually beat in the egg. Sift in the flour, cinnamon and nutmeg and fold into the mixture, alternating with the apple sauce. Spoon the mixture into the paper cases. Scatter the reserved topping over each cupcake to cover the tops and press down gently.

Bake in the preheated oven for 20 minutes, or until well risen and springy to the touch. Leave the cakes for 2–3 minutes in the tins before serving warm, or transfer to a wire rack to cool completely.

Lemon Meringue Cupcakes

makes 4

100 g/3½ oz butter, softened,
plus extra for greasing
100 g/3½ oz caster sugar
finely grated rind and juice of
½ lemon
1 large egg, lightly beaten
100 g/3½ oz self-raising flour,
sifted
2 tbsp lemon curd

meringue
2 egg whites
100 g/3½ oz caster sugar

Preheat the oven to 190°C/375°F/Gas Mark 5. Grease 4 x 200-ml/ 7-fl oz ramekins with butter.

Put the butter, sugar and lemon rind into a mixing bowl and beat together until light and fluffy. Gradually beat in the egg. Sift in the flour and, using a metal spoon, fold into the mixture with the lemon juice. Spoon the mixture into the ramekins.

Put the ramekins on a baking tray and bake in the preheated oven for 15 minutes, or until well risen and springy to the touch.

While the cupcakes are baking, make the meringue. Put the egg whites in a clean grease-free bowl and, using a hand-held electric mixer, mix until stiff. Gradually whisk in the sugar to form a stiff and glossy meringue.

When the cupcakes are cooked, remove from the oven. Spread the lemon curd over the hot cupcakes, then swirl over the meringue. Return the cupcakes to the oven for 4–5 minutes, until the meringue is golden. Serve immediately.

Spiced Plum Cupcakes

makes 4

55 g/2 oz butter, softened, plus extra for greasing

55 g/2 oz caster sugar

1 large egg, lightly beaten

55 g/2 oz plain wholemeal flour

½ tsp baking powder

1 tsp ground mixed spice

25 g/1 oz blanched hazelnuts, coarsely ground

2 small plums, halved, stoned and sliced

Preheat the oven to 180°C/350°F/Gas Mark 4. Grease 4 x 150-ml/5-fl oz ramekins with butter.

Put the butter and sugar in a bowl and beat together until light and fluffy. Gradually beat in the egg. Sift in the flour, baking powder and mixed spice (tipping any bran left in the sieve into the bowl) and, using a metal spoon, fold into the mixture with the ground hazelnuts. Spoon the mixture into the ramekins. Arrange the sliced plums on top of the mixture.

Put the ramekins on a baking sheet and bake in the preheated oven for 25 minutes, or until well risen and firm to the touch.

Tropical Pineapple Cupcakes

makes 12

2 slices canned pineapple in natural juice
85 g/3 oz butter, softened, or soft margarine
85 g/3 oz caster sugar
1 large egg, lightly beaten
85 g/3 oz self-raising flour

frosting
25 g/1 oz butter, softened
100 g/3½ oz soft cream cheese
grated rind of 1 lemon or lime
100 g/3½ oz icing sugar
1 tsp lemon or lime juice

Preheat the oven to 180°C/350°F/Gas Mark 4. Put 12 paper baking cases in a bun tin or put 12 double-layer paper cases on a baking tray.

Drain the pineapple, reserving the juice. Finely chop the pineapple slices. Place the butter and sugar in a large bowl and beat together until light and fluffy, then gradually beat in the egg. Add the flour and fold into the mixture. Fold in the chopped pineapple and 1 tablespoon of the reserved pineapple juice. Spoon the mixture into the paper cases.

Bake in the preheated oven for 20 minutes, or until well risen and springy to the touch. Transfer to a wire rack to cool completely.

To make the frosting, place the butter and cream cheese in a large bowl and beat together until smooth, then add the lemon rind.

Sift the icing sugar into the mixture and beat together until well mixed. Gradually beat in the lemon juice, adding enough to form a spreading consistency.

When the cupcakes are cold, spread the frosting on top of each cake, or fill a piping bag fitted with a large star nozzle and pipe the frosting on top.

Coconut Cherry Cupcakes

makes 12

115 g/4 oz butter, softened,
or soft margarine

115 g/4 oz caster sugar

2 tbsp milk

2 eggs, lightly beaten

85 g/3 oz self-raising flour

½ tsp baking powder

85 g/3 oz desiccated coconut

115 g/4 oz glacé cherries,
quartered

12 whole glacé, maraschino or
fresh cherries, to decorate

frosting

55 g/2 oz butter, softened

115 g/4 oz icing sugar

1 tbsp milk

Preheat the oven to 180°C/350°F/Gas Mark 4. Put 12 paper baking cases in a bun tin or put 12 double-layer paper cases on a baking tray.

Place the butter and sugar in a large bowl and beat together until light and fluffy. Stir in the milk and then gradually beat in the eggs. Sift in the flour and baking powder and fold them in with the coconut. Gently fold in most of the quartered cherries.

Spoon the mixture into the paper cases and scatter the remaining quartered cherries evenly on top.

Bake in the preheated oven for 20–25 minutes, or until well risen and springy to the touch. Transfer to a wire rack to cool completely.

To make the buttercream frosting, put the butter in a bowl and beat until light and fluffy. Sift in the icing sugar and beat together until well mixed, gradually beating in the milk.

When the cupcakes are cold, place the frosting in a piping bag fitted with a large star nozzle and pipe the frosting on top of each cupcake, then add a cherry to decorate.

Pistachio Cupcakes with Tangy Lime Frosting

makes 16

85 g/3 oz unsalted pistachio nuts

115 g/4oz butter, softened

140 g/5 oz golden caster sugar

140 g/5 oz self-raising flour

2 eggs, lightly beaten

4 tbsp Greek-style yoghurt

1 tbsp chopped pistachio nuts

frosting

115 g/4 oz butter, softened

2 tbsp lime juice cordial

few drops green food colouring (optional)

200 g/7 oz icing sugar

Preheat the oven to 180°C/350°F/Gas Mark 4. Put 16 paper baking cases in 2 x 12-hole bun tins or put 16 double-layer paper cases on a baking tray.

Put the pistachio nuts in a food processor or blender and process for a few seconds until finely ground. Add the butter, sugar, flour, eggs and yoghurt and then process until evenly mixed. Spoon the mixture into the paper cases.

Bake the cupcakes in the preheated oven for 20–25 minutes, or until well risen and springy to the touch. Transfer to a wire rack and leave to cool completely.

To make the frosting, put the butter, lime cordial and food colouring (if using) in a bowl and beat until light and fluffy. Sift in the icing sugar and beat until smooth. Swirl the frosting over each cupcake and sprinkle with the chopped pistachio nuts.

Banana & Pecan Cupcakes

makes 24

225 g/8 oz plain flour
1¼ tsp baking powder
¼ tsp bicarbonate of soda
2 ripe bananas
115 g/4 oz butter, softened,
or soft margarine
115 g/4 oz caster sugar
⅓ tsp vanilla extract
2 eggs, lightly beaten
4 tbsp soured cream
55 g/2 oz pecan nuts, roughly
chopped
25 g/1 oz pecan nuts, finely
chopped, to decorate

frosting
115 g/4 oz butter, softened
115 g/4 oz icing sugar

Preheat the oven to 190°C/375°F/Gas Mark 5. Put 24 paper baking cases in 2 x 12-hole bun tins or put 24 double-layer paper cases on a baking tray.

Sift together the flour, baking powder and bicarbonate of soda. Place the bananas in a separate bowl and mash with a fork.

Place the butter, sugar and vanilla extract in a large bowl and beat together until light and fluffy, then gradually beat in the eggs. Stir in the mashed bananas and soured cream. Fold in the flour mixture and chopped nuts. Spoon the mixture into the paper cases.

Bake in the preheated oven for 20 minutes, or until well risen and springy to the touch. Transfer to a wire rack to cool completely.

To make the frosting, place the butter in a bowl and beat until light and fluffy. Sift in the icing sugar and mix together well. Spread the frosting on top of each cupcake and sprinkle with the finely chopped pecan nuts before serving.

Carrot & Orange Cupcakes

makes 12

115 g/4 oz butter, softened,
or soft margarine

115 g/4 oz soft light brown
sugar

finely grated rind and juice of
1 small orange

2 large eggs, lightly beaten

175 g/6 oz carrots, grated

25 g/1 oz walnut pieces,
roughly chopped

125 g/4½ oz plain flour

1 tsp ground mixed spice

1½ tsp baking powder

frosting

280 g/10 oz mascarpone
cheese

4 tbsp icing sugar

grated rind of 1 large orange

Preheat the oven to 180°C/350°F/Gas Mark 4. Put 12 paper muffin cases in a muffin tin or put 12 double-layer paper cases on a baking tray.

Place the butter, sugar and orange rind in a bowl and beat together until light and fluffy, then gradually beat in the eggs. Squeeze any excess liquid from the carrots and add to the mixture with the walnuts and orange juice. Stir until well mixed. Sift in the flour, mixed spice and baking powder and fold in. Spoon the mixture into the paper cases.

Bake in the preheated oven for 25 minutes, or until well risen and springy to the touch. Transfer to a wire rack to cool completely.

To make the frosting, place the mascarpone cheese, icing sugar and orange rind in a large bowl and beat together until they are well mixed.

When the cupcakes are cold, spread the frosting on top of each cupcake, swirling it with a round-bladed knife.

Festive Fancies

Birthday Party Cupcakes

makes 24

225 g/8 oz butter, softened, or soft margarine

225 g/8 oz caster sugar

4 eggs

225 g/8 oz self-raising flour

a variety of sweets and chocolates, sugar-coated chocolates, dried fruits, edible sugar flower shapes, cake decorating sprinkles, sugar strands and silver or gold dragées

various tubes of coloured writing icing

candles and candle holders (optional), to decorate

frosting

175 g/6 oz butter, softened

350 g/12 oz icing sugar

Preheat the oven to 180°C/350°F/Gas Mark 4. Put 24 paper baking cases in 2 x 12-hole bun tins or put 24 double-layer paper cases on a baking tray.

Place the butter, sugar, eggs and flour in a large bowl and beat together until just smooth. Spoon the mixture into the paper cases.

Bake in the preheated oven for 15–20 minutes, or until well risen and springy to the touch. Transfer to a wire rack to cool completely.

To make the frosting, place the butter in a bowl and beat until light and fluffy. Sift in the icing sugar and beat together until smooth and creamy. When the cupcakes are cold, spread the frosting on top of each cupcake, then decorate as you like and place a candle in the top of each, if using.

Valentine Heart Cupcakes

makes 6

85 g/3 oz butter, softened, or soft margarine

85 g/3 oz caster sugar

½ tsp vanilla extract

2 eggs, lightly beaten

70 g/2½ oz plain flour

1 tbsp cocoa powder

1 tsp baking powder

6 chocolate flowers, to decorate

marzipan hearts

icing sugar, for dusting

35 g/1¼ oz marzipan

red food colouring (liquid or paste)

topping

55 g/2 oz butter, softened

115 g/4 oz icing sugar

25 g/1 oz plain chocolate, melted

To make the hearts, line a baking sheet with baking paper and lightly dust with icing sugar. Knead the marzipan until pliable, then add a few drops of red colouring and knead until evenly coloured. Roll out the marzipan to a thickness of 5 mm/¼ inch on a surface dusted with icing sugar. Cut out 6 hearts with a small heart-shaped cutter and place on the sheet. Leave for 3–4 hours.

To make the cupcakes, preheat the oven to 180°C/350°F/ Gas Mark 4. Put 6 paper baking cases in a bun tin or put 6 double-layer paper cases on a baking tray.

Place the butter, sugar and vanilla extract in a large bowl and beat together until light and fluffy, then gradually beat in the eggs. Sift in the flour, cocoa powder and baking powder and fold into the mixture. Spoon the mixture into the paper cases.

Bake in the preheated oven for 20–25 minutes, or until well risen and springy to the touch. Transfer to a wire rack to cool completely.

To make the topping, place the butter in a bowl and beat until light and fluffy. Sift in the icing sugar and beat until smooth. Add the melted chocolate and beat until mixed. Spread the icing on top of each cupcake and decorate with a chocolate flower and a marzipan heart.

Easter Cupcakes

makes 12

115 g/4 oz butter, softened,
or soft margarine
115 g/4 oz caster sugar
2 eggs, lightly beaten
85 g/3 oz self-raising flour
25 g/1 oz cocoa powder
2 x 130-g/4¾-oz packets mini
sugar-coated chocolate eggs,
to decorate

frosting

85 g/3 oz butter, softened
175 g/6 oz icing sugar
1 tbsp milk
2–3 drops vanilla extract

Preheat the oven to 180°C/350°F/Gas Mark 4. Put 12 paper baking cases in a bun tin or put 12 double-layer paper cases on a baking tray.

Place the butter and sugar in a large bowl and beat together until light and fluffy, then gradually beat in the eggs. Sift in the flour and cocoa powder and fold into the mixture. Spoon the mixture into the paper cases.

Bake in the preheated oven for 15–20 minutes, or until well risen and springy to the touch. Transfer to a wire rack to cool completely.

To make the buttercream frosting, place the butter in a bowl and beat until light and fluffy. Sift in the icing sugar and beat together until well mixed, adding the milk and vanilla extract.

When the cupcakes are cold, place the frosting in a piping bag, fitted with a large star nozzle and pipe a circle around the edge of each cupcake to form a nest. Place chocolate eggs in the centre of each nest to decorate.

Baby Shower Cupcakes with Sugared Almonds

makes 24

400 g/14 oz butter, softened

400 g/14 oz caster sugar

finely grated rind of
2 lemons

8 eggs, lightly beaten

400 g/14 oz self-raising flour

24 sugared almonds,
to decorate

icing

350 g/12 oz icing sugar

6–8 tsp hot water

red or blue food colouring
(liquid or paste)

Preheat the oven to 180°C/350°F/Gas Mark 4. Put 24 paper baking cases in 2 x 12-hole bun tins or put 24 double-layer paper cases on a baking tray.

Place the butter, sugar and lemon rind in a large bowl and beat together until light and fluffy, then gradually beat in the eggs. Sift in the flour and fold into the mixture. Spoon the mixture into the paper cases.

Bake in the preheated oven for 20–25 minutes, or until well risen and springy to the touch. Transfer to a wire rack to cool completely.

When the cakes are cold, make the icing. Sift the icing sugar into a bowl, add the hot water and stir until smooth and thick enough to coat the back of a wooden spoon. Dip a skewer into the red or blue food colouring and stir it into the icing until it is evenly coloured pink or pale blue. Spoon the icing on top of each cupcake. Top each cupcake with a sugared almond and leave to set for about 30 minutes.

Spring-time Cupcakes

makes 24

150 g/5½ oz butter, softened,
or soft margarine
150 g/5½ oz caster sugar
1 tsp vanilla extract
2 large eggs, lightly beaten
140 g/5 oz self-raising flour
40 g/1½ oz cornflour
coloured sugar strands,
to decorate

icing
115 g/4 oz ready-to-roll
fondant icing
yellow and green food
colourings
300 g/10½ oz icing sugar
about 3 tbsp cold water

Preheat the oven to 190°C/375°F/Gas Mark 5. Put 24 paper baking cases in 2 x 12-hole bun tins or put 24 double-layer paper cases on a baking tray. Place the butter and sugar in a large bowl and beat together until light and fluffy, then beat in the vanilla extract. Gradually beat in the eggs. Sift in the flour and cornflour and fold into the mixture. Spoon the mixture into the paper cases.

Bake in the preheated oven for 12–15 minutes, or until well risen and springy to the touch. Transfer to a wire rack to cool completely.

To make the icing, divide the fondant in half and colour one half pale yellow. Roll out both halves, then use the sides of a round pastry cutter to cut out white and yellow petal shapes. Set aside.

Sift the icing sugar into a bowl and mix with the water until smooth. Place half of the icing in a small piping bag fitted with a small plain nozzle. Divide the remaining icing in half and colour one portion yellow and the other green.

Cover 12 cupcakes with yellow icing and 12 with green icing. Arrange white petals on top of the yellow icing to form flowers. Pipe a little blob of white icing into the centre of each flower, then sprinkle a few coloured sugar strands on top of the white icing to form the centre of the flower. Arrange the yellow petals on the green icing and decorate in the same way. Leave to set.

Halloween Cupcakes

makes 12

115 g/4 oz butter, softened,
or soft margarine

115 g/4 oz caster sugar

2 eggs

115 g/4 oz self-raising flour

icing

200 g/7 oz orange ready-to-
roll coloured fondant icing

icing sugar, for dusting

55 g/2 oz black ready-to-roll
coloured fondant icing

black writing icing

white writing icing

Preheat the oven to 180°C/350°F/Gas Mark 4. Put 12 paper baking cases in a bun tin or put 12 double-layer paper cases on a baking tray.

Place the butter, sugar, eggs and flour in a large bowl and beat together until smooth. Spoon the mixture into the paper cases.

Bake in the preheated oven for 15–20 minutes, or until well risen and springy to the touch. Transfer to a wire rack to cool completely.

When the cupcakes are cold, knead the orange icing until pliable, then roll out on a surface dusted with icing sugar. Rub icing sugar into the icing to prevent it from spotting.

Cut out 12 circles with a 5.5-cm/2¼-inch round cutter, re-rolling the icing as necessary. Place a circle on top of each cupcake.

Roll out the black icing on a surface dusted with icing sugar. Rub icing sugar into the icing to prevent spotting. Cut out 12 circles with a 3-cm/1¼-inch round cutter and place them in the centre of the cupcake. Using black writing icing, pipe 8 legs onto each spider and draw eyes and a mouth with white writing icing. Leave to set.

Christmas Cupcakes

makes 12

125 g/4½ oz butter, softened
200 g/7 oz caster sugar
4–6 drops almond extract
4 eggs, lightly beaten
150 g/5½ oz self-raising flour
175 g/6 oz ground almonds

topping

450 g/1 lb white ready-to-roll
fondant icing
icing sugar, for dusting
55 g/2 oz green
ready-to-roll coloured
fondant icing
25 g/1 oz red ready-to-roll
coloured fondant icing

Preheat the oven to 180°C/350°F/Gas Mark 4. Put 12 paper baking cases in a bun tin or put 12 double-layer paper cases on a baking tray.

Place the butter, sugar and almond extract in a large bowl and beat together until light and fluffy, then gradually beat in the eggs. Sift in the flour and fold into the mixture, then fold in the ground almonds. Spoon the mixture into the paper cases.

Bake in the preheated oven for 20 minutes, or until well risen and springy to the touch. Transfer to a wire rack to cool completely.

When the cupcakes are cold, knead the white icing until pliable, then roll out on a surface lightly dusted with icing sugar. Cut out 12 circles with a 7-cm/2¾-inch plain round cutter, re-rolling the icing as necessary. Place a circle on top of each cupcake.

Roll out the green icing on a surface lightly dusted with icing sugar. Rub icing sugar into the icing to prevent it from spotting. Cut out 24 leaves with a holly leaf-shaped cutter, re-rolling the icing as necessary. Brush each leaf with a little cooled boiled water and place 2 leaves on top of each cupcake. Roll the red icing between the palms of your hands to form 36 berries and place 3 in the centre of the leaves on each cupcake, to decorate.

Festive Cupcakes

makes 14

115 g/4 oz mixed dried fruit
1 tsp finely grated orange rind
2 tbsp brandy or orange juice
85 g/3 oz butter, softened
85 g/3 oz light soft brown sugar
1 large egg, lightly beaten
115 g/4 oz self-raising flour
1 tsp ground mixed spice
1 tbsp silver dragées, to decorate

icing
85 g/3 oz icing sugar
2 tbsp orange juice

Put the mixed fruit, orange rind and brandy or orange juice in a small bowl and cover and leave to soak for 1 hour.

Preheat the oven to 190°C/375°F/Gas Mark 5. Put 14 paper baking cases in 2 x 12-hole bun tins or put 14 double-layer paper cases on a baking tray.

Put the butter and sugar in a mixing bowl and beat together until light and fluffy. Gradually beat in the egg. Sift in the flour and mixed spice and, using a metal spoon, fold them into the mixture followed by the soaked fruit. Spoon the mixture into the paper cases.

Bake the cupcakes in the preheated oven for 15–20 minutes, or until well risen and springy to the touch. Transfer to a cooling rack and leave to cool completely.

To make the icing, sift the icing sugar into a bowl and gradually mix in enough orange juice until the mixture is smooth and thick enough to coat the back of a wooden spoon. Using a teaspoon, drizzle the icing in a ziz-zag pattern over the cupcakes. Decorate with the silver dragées. Leave to set.

Wedding Day Fancy Favours

makes 12

115 g/4 oz butter, softened
100 g/3½ oz caster sugar
2 eggs, lightly beaten
140 g/5 oz self-raising flour, sifted
½ tsp vanilla extract
1–2 tbsp milk

topping
icing sugar, for dusting
225 g/8oz white ready-to-roll fondant icing
3 tbsp runny honey, warmed
2–3 drops pink food colouring
tube of green writing icing

Preheat the oven to 200°C/400°F/Gas Mark 6. Put 12 paper baking cases in a muffin tin or put 12 double-layer paper cases on a baking tray.

Place the butter and caster sugar into a mixing bowl and beat together for 1–2 minutes, until pale and creamy. Gradually add the eggs and continue beating. Fold in the flour using a metal spoon. Stir in the vanilla extract and milk.

Spoon the mixture into the paper cases. Bake in the preheated oven for 15-20 minutes, or until well risen and springy to the touch. Remove from the oven and leave to cool for 5 minutes in the tin, then move the cupcakes to a wire rack to cool completely.

Dust the work surface with some icing sugar. Roll out all but one eighth of the fondant icing to 20 x 28 cm/8 x 11 inches. Use a biscuit cutter to stamp out 12 rounds. Brush the cake tops with some honey and stick on the rounds.

For the rosebuds, knead the remaining icing with the food colouring. Rub icing sugar into the icing to prevent it from spotting. Roll out 12 strips of icing to 1 x 6 cm/½ x 2½ inch. Roll up from one end and stick onto the cake with a dab of honey. Draw on a stalk and leaves with the writing icing. Leave to set.

Gold & Silver Anniversary Cupcakes

makes 24

225 g/8 oz butter, softened
225 g/8 oz caster sugar
1 tsp vanilla extract
4 large eggs, lightly beaten
225 g/8 oz self-raising flour
5 tbsp milk
25 g/1 oz silver or gold
dragées, to decorate

frosting
175 g/6 oz butter
350 g/12 oz icing sugar

Preheat the oven to 180°C/350°F/Gas Mark 4. Put 24 paper baking cases in 2 x 12-hole bun tins or put 24 double-layer paper cases on a baking tray.

Place the butter, sugar and vanilla extract in a large bowl and beat together until light and fluffy, then gradually beat in the eggs. Sift in the flour and fold into the mixture with the milk. Spoon the mixture into the paper cases.

Bake in the preheated oven for 15–20 minutes, or until well risen and springy to the touch. Transfer to a wire rack to cool completely.

To make the frosting, place the butter in a large bowl and beat until light and fluffy. Sift in the icing sugar and beat together until well mixed. Place the frosting in a piping bag fitted with a medium star-shaped nozzle.

When the cupcakes are cold, pipe circles of frosting on top of each cake to cover the tops and sprinkle over the silver or gold dragées.